MW01034356

An Essay on the
Not-self, Nothingness,
and Being
of Consciousness

# An Essay on the Not-self, Nothingness, and Being of Consciousness

*A Primer on Existential Buddhism*

Dr. Armando S. Garcia

*To*
*The love of my life,*
*my wife Sandra*
*and*
*to the joys of my life,*
*my children Arthur and Samantha*

# Table of Contents

# Preface

Is there a Self?

Is the Self an illusion?

Is there a real person that is conscious?

What am I? Who am I?

Although seemingly inconsequential, on these questions hinge over two thousand years of eastern and western philosophical thought. These are questions that we, either consciously or subconsciously, are confronted with whenever we examine our thoughts and beliefs, when we are bored, or in times of distress. For these are existential questions that originate from the very essence of human consciousness.

How we see ourselves determines how we react to the world. If we believe we are spiritual beings, then we see the world through the sacred, aspire to a life beyond this earth, and value the ethical, the mystical, the self-sacrifice. If we see ourselves as manifestations of the physical, then we value pleasure, materials, and the here and now. If we see ourselves as emptiness, then we look to unity and harmony as our purpose.

Yet, all the ways we have of seeing our Self particularly reflect our inherent amblyopia in our Self-perception. It is because we cannot truly see who, or what, we are, that we create our-selves in many ways. But the problem is not that we lack essence, but rather that we look for it in the wrong way and in the wrong place.

Eleven years ago, when I was intensely practicing Buddhist mediation, I arrived at an impasse. I was able to meditate to the point where all my thoughts and physical perceptions would cease; yet no matter how long I dwelled in this deep state of concentration meditation, I was always aware of being aware, always aware of myself as being a point of view. This was a problem because the Not-self doctrine of the Buddha, and commentaries and teachings on the subject, insist on the illusion of the self, denying the existence of any individual or person at the origin of self-consciousness:

> *There is no specific entity in anything. That is emptiness. That is the nothingness. That nothingness is also experienced in meditation. It is empty, it is devoid of a specific person, devoid of a specific thing, devoid of anything which makes it permanent, devoid of anything which even makes it important. The whole thing is in flux. So the emptiness is that. And the emptiness is to be seen everywhere; to be seen in*

*oneself. And that is what is called anatta, non-self. Empty of an entity... There is continuity, but there is no special entity. And that continuity is what makes it so difficult for us to see that there really isn't anybody inside the body making things happen. (Khema 1984)*

Buddhist psychology describes the self as constituted of five aggregates (the khandhas in Pali, Skandhas in Sanskrit), which are described as impermanent and not a self:

*Thus, monks, any form whatsoever that is past, future, or present; internal or external; blatant or subtle; common or sublime; far or near: every form is to be seen as it actually is with right discernment as: 'This is not mine. This is not my self. This is not what I am.'*

*Any feeling whatsoever...*

*Any perception whatsoever...*

*Any fabrications whatsoever...*

*Any consciousness whatsoever that is past, future, or present; internal or external; blatant or subtle; common or sublime; far or near: every consciousness is to be seen as it actually is with right discernment as: 'This is not mine. This is not my self. This is not what I am.' (SN 22.59) (See appendix)*

That the aggregates are not a self means that anything which I can perceive is not what I am—and that includes everything. But then who is it that is doing the perceiving? If the self which is having the experience is an illusion, then how can an illusion observe itself to be an illusion? How can an impermanent consciousness experience its own impermanence? How can consciousness be nothing?

After further intense and prolonged effort it became clear that even if I reached the ultimate state of meditation concentration, the dimension of nothingness, there would still be a consciousness knowing that that state was being experienced, or otherwise it would have to be an unconsciousness:

> *I tell you, the ending of the mental fermentations depends on the first jhana... the second jhana... the third... the fourth... the dimension of the infinitude of space... the dimension of the infinitude of consciousness... the dimension of nothingness. (Access to Insight. 2013)*

I could see no possible way that I could experience not having a point of view, experience being No-self, experience being nothing.

My first impression of Jean Paul Sartre's opus magnum, *Being and Nothingness*, was near mystical; that is, in some obscure way I almost understood what he said. However, after being able to meditate to the point of no perception, his book made perfect sense. Both Buddhism and Existentialism are referring to the same experience of awareness, as Not-self and Nothingness.

Consciousness is not anything, and it is everything. Not being anything, it is empty, and everything in it is therefore empty. The illusion is the rational Self, which we create out of the world, out of our need to be some-thing. There is necessarily always a point of view: The Being that is an absolute subjectivity.

Human consciousness is Being. The philosopher Martin Heidegger described Being—capitalized to indicate human being—as that being that is conscious of its own existence and is aware of the existence of other beings. When Being realizes not being the Self, it becomes enlightened.

This book explains how we are at once Not-self, Nothingness, and Being.

# Introduction

Unique to Buddhism is the doctrine of Not-self. Unique to Existentialism is the concept of Nothingness. As Not-self and as Nothingness, consciousness is not like anything else. However, when the conscious experience is conceived as a phenomenon, then Not-self is misunderstood as Non-being, and Nothingness is reduced to absurdity. Consciousness is an existing, a presence, a positivity, a Being, and not any-thing.

The Nothingness, the Not-self, of consciousness affects our entire existence as self-conscious beings. It conditions the emergence of the Self, feeds our desire for the World, and it is the fount of our deepest fears. We are self-conscious because we are not anything, because we are a nihilation of the world of things. And although not being anything endows us with absolute freedom, with free will, for most of us it becomes rather a source of existential dread.

Imperative to the understanding of Buddhism is the realization of the Not-self doctrine. Because we experience the world essentially as Not-self, it is also impermanent and not satisfying. Consequently, any identification with the world as a self will inevitably lead to frustration and suffering. And although there is plenty of literature regarding the nature of the self and how get rid of it, there is little comment as to what is left in the aftermath of its demise. The general understanding is that to realize Nibbana (or Nirvana), any identification as a self must be eliminated; yet the teachings are nebulous as to what has been attained, and who gets to enjoy it, since there is no one left there, there. Conceived in this way, the Not-self doctrine becomes a doctrine of No-self and a proposition pregnant with contradictions. The Not-self doctrine as originally expounded by the Buddha, however, is profound and perfect, and generally misunderstood.

Existentialism is a vague designation applied to the ideas of philosophers and artists from the late 19th to mid-20th century whose works explored the experience of existing. Although encompassing the output of many philosophers, writers, artists, and musicians, preeminent have been the philosophical works of Husserl, Heidegger, and Sartre in establishing its fundamental principles. In his

major work, *Being and Nothingness*, Jean Paul Sartre
(b.1905, d.1980) distills the ideas of his predecessors in formulating his original concepts regarding
the Nothingness of consciousness. Fundamental
to his thesis is the characterization of human consciousness as "existence before essence," and in so
doing left human awareness suspended in absurdity. Heidegger elaborated profoundly on Being
(capitalized to indicate human awareness) as being
the essence of human existence; yet the breadth of
this insight has been appreciated by few. The
Nothingness without Being is reduced to nihilism.

Although the title of this book appears over-
ambitious, the goal is to succinctly establish the
fundamental principle that makes Buddhism and
Existentialism congruent and more comprehensi-
ble: that the Nothingness and Not-self of human
consciousness is experienced as Being. And to this
extent, it establishes the foundation for an Existential Buddhism.

Human Being is a particular awareness of existing; it is a particularly human way of being conscious. As Being, existing is knowing, knowing is
existing: It is all action. What we are as knowing
beings, we cannot know: We are blind to it because
we are *it*. It cannot be spoken about without falling
into error because words are already objects of
consciousness and not the Being-itself. As a result,

the Buddha wisely referred to this Being as Not-self. It is in this sense that Being is at once a Nothingness, an Emptiness, and a Fullness.

# Not-self and Nothingness

I t was during his second discourse after his enlightenment, when Gautama the Buddha revealed the nature of human existence as character-
ized by impermanence, dissatisfaction, and as not-
self. Yet despite two and a half millennia since the
exposition of his profound insight, the Not-self
doctrine continues to be a source of disagreement,
misunderstanding, and a motive for the rejection
of Buddhism. The source of this confusion lies not
with any deficiency of the doctrine, but in that it
points to a reality which exists beyond the limits of
rational description.

The perplexity in understanding the Not-self
doctrine hinges on the conceptualization of the
self that is negated.

During the genesis of Buddhism, Gautama the
Buddha was contending with the Hindu belief in a
true self or soul: the atman. It was thought to be
the essence of a person, which transcends the

physical body and the mind (consciousness) and is one with Brahman (the ultimate principle of existence). The Buddha denied the existence of the Hindu true self or soul (the atman) because during his practice of asceticism, despite arduous and torturous efforts, he could not experience it. He declared, instead, that the self is comprised of qualities, or aggregates, which are ultimately impermanent and a cause of suffering.

In Buddhist psychology, the self, or ego, is conceptualized as constituted by what are called the five Khandhas (in Pali), or Skhandhas (in Sanskrit), also called the aggregates, namely: the forms, feelings, perceptions, mental formations, and consciousness. These khandhas manifest when consciousness makes contact with the physical world. The contact of an object with the senses produces sense consciousness and conscious feelings of either pleasure or pain (or neutral feelings), which then give rise to perceptions (what it is), and finally mental formations (ideas and intentions) regarding the experienced object. These are considered impermanent by the Theravada school and empty by the Mahayana schools of Buddhism.

The Mahayana based schools interpret the self as a conditioned entity with no substance. They consider self-consciousness as dependent on the universe for its existence and therefore an illusion with no individual entity. For this school of thought, liberation (Nirvana) consists in the realization of the absolute emptiness of all phenomena, or *sunyata:*

> *The Buddha teaches that, what we call ego, self, soul, personality etc., are merely conventional terms not referring to any real independent entity. And he teaches that there is only to be found this psychophysical process of existence changing from moment to moment. Without understanding the egolessness of existence, it is not possible to gain a real understanding of the Buddha-word; and it is not possible without it to realize that goal of emancipation and deliverance of mind proclaimed by the Buddha . . . Whoso, however, has fully penetrated the egolessness of existence, knows that, in the highest sense, there is no individual that suffers, that commits the kammic deeds, that enters Nirvana, and that brings the Eightfold Path to perfection. (Thera 2013)*

The Buddhist Theravada school of thought consider the realization of the Not-self doctrine (*Anatta-lakkhana Sutta*) as the basis for liberation (Nibbana). It is the transcendence of all aspects of self-perception, at the very roots of the psyche, which attains enlightenment. While most Theravada pundits interpret anatta as no-self, as the absence of any individual entity, others feel that this was not the intention of Gautama the Buddha. The Theravada scholar Thanissaro Bhikkhu explains that the Not-self doctrine is rather a "not-self strategy," reasoning that the Buddha never gave an answer when questioned as to the existence of an individual self, and because the question itself is one that should be "put aside," as it does not contribute to the liberation from suffering and may instead lead to confusion (Bhikkhu 1996).

In the western cultures, the self, or ego, is widely understood as totality of the physical and mental properties which constitute a person. The answer to the question "who are you?" will typically involve a name, age, occupation, marital status, childhood history, ethnic background, and the physical characteristics of body (size and shape, skin and hair color, eye color, etcetera); that is, some narrative regarding one's perception of the body, feelings, emotions, and thoughts. Modern psychology considers the self to be an illusion, an epiphenomenon of the brain, an evolutionary solution.

Whether we consider the self as comprised of ideas or the khandas, it is generally considered to be an illusion by both easterner and western modern thinkers. But if the self consists of impermanent khandas, then who is the one perceiving them as such? And If the self is made of thoughts, then who is the one thinking them?

With some practice in introspection, it is not too difficult to determine the impermanence of the first four khandhas. There is a problem, however, when considering the impermanence of con-sciousness:

> *Impermanence (anicca) may appear obvious to some who see the gross origin and disappearance of ani-mate and inanimate entities. However, the Buddha's teaching goes beyond the gross and obvious and ex-tends also to the mind, including its most subtle and sublime level... "whatever consciousness, past, future or present, internal or external, coarse or fine, low or lofty, far or near, all that consciousness must be re-garded with proper wisdom, according to reality, thus: 'This is not mine, this I am not, this is not my self.'* (Mendis 1979)

For then, if consciousness is an impermanent khandha, then there is a consciousness which is aware of its own impermanence, or its own other-ness. One could easily formulate a theory of the impermanence of consciousness, but how could this be experienced? No matter how this theory is contrived, there would always be an impermanent consciousness observing its own impermanence or otherness: a contradiction.

9

Similarly, if the ego is composed of thoughts and emotions, then there must be a consciousness which is aware and makes sense, that connects, the stream of thoughts, and if that consciousness were the thoughts, then there would be an infinite regression of thoughts perceiving thoughts: a contradiction.

It appears then that with both Western and Buddhist perceptions of the self we have lost the perceiver, the one who knows, the one who is aware. We have relied so much on thinking and reasoning as a way of being that we have lost sight of the Thinker: to the general mind, the thoughts are the Thinker. The famous psychologist Carl Jung had this observation:

> *The psyche is the greatest of all cosmic wonders and the "sine qua non" of the world as an object. It is in the highest degree odd that Western man, with but very few—and ever fewer- exceptions, apparently pays so little regard to this fact. Swamped by the knowledge of external objects, the subject of all knowledge has been temporarily eclipsed to the point of seeming nonexistence. (Jung 1960, 77)*

The confusion lies with the conceptualization of the Self. Is the Self the consciousness itself or is it an object of consciousness? Is the Self the one who thinks or is it the thoughts?

10

We require a new perspective to unravel the conundrum of the Not-self of consciousness.

During the mid-20th century, a group of philosophers, now called the Existentialists, addressed the study of consciousness from a subjective point of view rather than by logical reasoning. They proposed to investigate the experience of being conscious.

The popular notion is that we have a mind, in the body, looking out at a physical world which we directly experience through the senses: we see, hear, taste, touch, and smell a real world. However, this is not the case. For example, what we identify as a red apple is an image projected by the lens of the eye on the retina (inverted), which then stimulates the cone and rod receptor cells of the retina to produce chemical substances, which stimulate nerves to transmit a chemical signal to the visual cortex area of the brain, where this information is reconstructed (somehow) into the conscious image of the red apple. In the same manner, we do not hear actual sound waves but experience the effect the sound waves have on the hearing apparatus, which is then transmitted by nerve signals, which are then experienced as the phenomenon of sound. The same mechanism is true for taste, smell, and touch. What we consciously experience is all stimulation of nerve endings. We can never get beyond our sense perception in knowing the physical world; the only reality we truly know is the "impression" the senses produce on our consciousness, or the conscious impressions. In other words, the world, as we know it, is made of consciousness.

To investigate the problem of the conscious perception of the world, the philosopher Edmund Husserl (b.1859, d.1938) developed a discipline he called Phenomenology. He wanted to arrive at a direct experience of conscious perception, one that was not contaminated by any logic or thinking. This was of particular importance for scientific investigation, which aims at making objective observations. The phenomenon, Husserl determined, is the series of appearances produced by the "existents" (the things we cannot get at with our senses) as they manifest in a consciousness. All we experience, he found, is the effect sense perception has on consciousness. Fortunately, the phenomena portray the existents very accurately: "The phenomenon can be studied and described as such, for it is *absolutely indicative of itself*. . . the being of an existent is exactly what it *appears*" (Sartre 1984, 4). As a result, the division of an inside consciousness and on outside world is reduced to a perceiving consciousness and the conscious impressions:

"The reflecting consciousness posits the consciousness reflected-on, as its object" (Sartre 1984, 12). In other words, there is no inside mind and outside world, but the rather the world is in the mind. Sartre observed that if the perceiving-consciousness were the consciousness-perceived then it would be an unconscious perception, or a contradiction:

*for if my consciousness were not consciousness of being consciousness of the table, it would then be consciousness of that table without consciousness of being so. In other words, it would be a consciousness ignorant of itself, an unconscious--which is absurd. (Sartre 1984, 11)*

Therefore, there must be a consciousness which is consciousness of itself as it is conscious of its objects of consciousness. Furthermore, Sartre adds, the knower must know itself "directly" in the act of knowing:

*Consciousness of self is not dual. If we wish to avoid an infinite regress, there must be an immediate, non-cognitive relation of the self to itself . . . every positional consciousness of an object is at the same time a non-positional consciousness of itself. (Sartre 1984, 12-13)*

This consciousness, which knows itself in the act of knowing, is referred to by philosophers as the *pre-reflective consciousness* (also the non-reflective consciousness). It is due to the overindulged habit of reflective thinking that makes it difficult to conceive of knowing without words:

> *consciousness is the knowing being in his capacity as being and not as being known. This means that we must abandon the primacy of knowledge if we wish to establish that knowledge. (Sartre 1989, 11)*

It is evident, for example, that even young infants are aware of the otherness of the objects they observe (have a pre-reflective awareness); for otherwise, like the animals, they would be completely identified with the environment and hence unable to learn from it. Sartre further states in this regard:

> *Thus reflection has no kind of primacy over the consciousness reflected-on. It is not reflection which reveals the consciousness reflected-on to itself. Quite the contrary, it is the non-reflective consciousness which renders the reflection possible; there is a pre-reflective cogito which is the condition of the Cartesian cogito. (Sartre 1984, 13)*

Meaning that the pre-reflective consciousness, or *direct knowing*, is not a proto-consciousness or an un-consciousness: It is the basis for all consciousness experience. The Self, or Ego, is the "reflection" of the pre-reflective consciousness. This direct knowing has been referred to by Buddhist as the

Original Mind, also called No-mind, and what the Theravada master Ajahn Cha calls "the One Who Knows" (Ajahn Cha 2002).

The pre-reflective consciousness cannot itself be an object of awareness because it is the awareness. It is, in this respect, an *absolute subjectivity*. What is commonly referred to as "self-consciousness" is the ability of the awareness (the pre-reflective consciousness) to create an image for itself with the objects of consciousness, to dress itself with the thoughts of the world. Because this pre-reflective awareness is an absolute subjectivity, it is as if transparent to itself. It is like the wind, only to be revealed when it moves something.

Although we do many things without thinking about it, like putting on clothes, walking, and even driving, in the day-to-day experience of most persons, the pre-reflective consciousness exceptionally becomes conspicuous. It is the fabricated Self which we generally identify with our existence, our being.

From the point of view of reflection, from the point of view of the reflected Self, the knower seems non-existent:

> *The knower is not; he is not apprehensible. He is nothing other than that which brings it about that there is a being-there on the part of the known, a presence.* (Sartre 1984, 246)

15

Because we cannot see what we are, because we are a No-thingness in relation to the things of the world, we create the Self through our thinking; we create a reflection, an idea of who we think we are. Everything which we can observe as an object of consciousness, everything which we can experience objectively, which includes not only the physical objects and the body but also our thoughts, perceptions, and emotions, we will designate as the World. We are not the World. The self which we create from the World, which we can perceive objectively, we will designate as the Self. This is the Self that we generally refer to when saying we are "self-conscious." This is the Self that has no inherent existence, that can be taken apart like a cart or a puzzle. This is the Self that we are Not. It is from this perspective that the statement "this is not mine, this I am not, this is not my self" is intelligible and not contradictory.

Ultimately, the only accurate way of expressing the Knower, the One Who Knows, is as Not-self, as any description would be a reflection (an idea) and not the *thing-in-itself*. This Not-self does not designate non-being, nor a non-individual, but is a descriptive term for not-being-any-thing-which-we-can-name. In this sense Nothingness and Not Self have the same origin, the same being. Thus,

16

the Not-self doctrine of the Buddha is most complete and exact. The confusion comes from interpreting Not-self as a metaphysical doctrine, rather than the practical guide, the "not-self strategy," for the elimination of suffering, as was intended.

We have thus far established that we are not anything which is an object of our awareness, that we are not the Self, that we are a No-thingness, that we are a transparent pre-reflective consciousness; but this still leaves us with nothing, with negations. We still do not know who or what we are.

Sartre arrives at the Nothingness by examining the questioning being. It is by questioning the world, Sartre points out, that the human being comes to understand its own being. In this respect, it is the capacity of the non-reflective consciousness to maintain an objective point of view, to create a *distance* between itself and the objects of consciousness, that allows for a perspective from which to question. And to do this, consciousness must be *absolutely* outside of the World it looks upon. Sartre denotes this as the "nihilating power" of consciousness. This nihilation of the World from its being allows it to question, to apprehend a negative answer, and to ascertain the possibility of not-being:

> *this appearance of the self beyond the world—that is, beyond the totality of the real—is an emergence of 'human reality' in nothingness.* (Sartre 1984, 51)

From a rational point of view, self-conscious being comes into existence through a *nihilation* of the world of beings. Sartre describes being, or existence, as consisting of consciousness, or being-For-itself, and everything else as the being-In-itself. The For-itself gives meaning, existence, to the In-itself, and in turn it uses the In-itself to fashion being for itself. Sartre denies the For-itself a plenitude of existence. He determines the For-itself as dependent on the In-itself for its being: "All consciousness, as Husserl has shown, is consciousness *of* something" (1989, 11). From the point of view of reasoning, of reflection, the pre-reflective consciousness does not appear as anything, as it has no in-itself. From the point of view of meditation, however, a different perspective emerges.

In the practice of concentration meditation, the mind uses one object as a focus of attention, usually the breathing, to release all other conscious perceptions. Then, as the mind enters the state called *absorption*, or Jahna, even the awareness of breathing fades away, leaving only an awareness of being awareness. Indeed, if all consciousness were

18

"a consciousness of something," it would be impossible to do concentration meditation since the mind would be bound to its objects. Just as vision is defined as the "seeing of something," and seeing in total darkness is not blindness, so is the pre-reflective consciousness able to be aware of being awareness. Gautama the Buddha pronounced this unconditioned state (i.e., the non-reflective consciousness) in the well-known passage of this Sutta:

> *There is, monks, an unborn, unbecome, unmade, unconditioned. If, monks, there were no unborn, unbecome, unmade, unconditioned, no escape would be discerned from what is born, become, made, conditioned. (Ud 8.3) (Bodhi 2005, 366)*

Consciousness, as a transparent absolute subjectivity, is unconditioned; it is a Knowing which knows itself knowing but not as known; it is Being.

Being is more than consciousness, more than awareness, more than a knowing; it is foremost a certitude of existing, an actualization. The concept of Being, or existence, originates with the ancient Greek philosophers but was forgotten, or ignored, for two thousand years until the German philosopher Martin Heidegger (b.1889, d1976) brought it to modern consciousness. In his major work, *Being and Time*, he describes at great length the essential-

ity of the Being (capitalized to indicate human being) that is concerned with being, concerned with
existence.

As what could be called the principle of Apper-
ceptive Opacity, we find that the closer an entity is
to us, the less evident it becomes to our apprehension; so that as we recede from town, to neighbor-
hood, to home, to family, and to the body, our perceptions become increasingly opaque, so that we
are complete imperceptive to what is most intrin-
sically us, our very Being. So all-encompassing and
thoroughly conspicuous is our Being, that in the
efforts of humankind to understand the physical
universe, the very origin of understanding, the observing Being, has gone undetected; it has been as-
sumed until recently that our observations are her-
metic to the effect of the observer.

We are now able to assert what the Buddha was
pointing to with the Not-self doctrine. The use of
any term or words to describe awareness (the non-
reflective consciousness) would immediately determine it an object of consciousness, an idea, and
thwart any possibility of direct knowing. Indubita-
bly, all conscious perceptions must have a perceiver, a knower. What Edmund Husserl meant,
although awkwardly, by "consciousness is always a
consciousness of something" is that all observa-

tions are from a subjective point of view, a subjective consciousness, or what he also called "intentionality." Every observation involves a questioning Being. Which means that no one, not even the Buddha, could possibly observe their nonexistence.

The rest of the book will examine how human consciousness reveals itself as a Not-self, a Nothingness, and a fullness of Being.

# The Self and the Other

If it were possible for someone to mature without other persons, how would such a mind manifest? Without others to communicate with, there would be no need for language, and without language there would be no conceptual thinking. Thus, the only consciousness that would manifest would be the non-reflective consciousness: a non-reflective self-awareness. Without a reflective consciousness, there would be no emergence of a Self. Without a sense of Self, there would be no suffering. Would this then be an enlightened being? Is the Self, superfluous?

Although we are essentially Not-self, we nevertheless depend on a Self to interact with each other in the world. Yet this interaction between self and others is everything but simple.

Sartre begins his evaluation of the Other by considering the situation of a man spying through a keyhole. In his immediate present, in his aloneness, absorbed in his action of spying, he is not reflecting, not thinking. He is not his Self but only pure non-reflective consciousness:

> *there is no self to inhabit my consciousness...I am my acts...I am pure consciousness of things...I cannot truly define myself as being in a situation: first because I am not a positional consciousness of myself; second because I am my own nothingness. (Sartre 1984, 347-48)*

But now he hears approaching footsteps, and suddenly he becomes aware of his shameful act; he becomes a voyeur. The sudden apprehension of the possibility of being seen makes the nothingness of his consciousness a *somethingness*, an object for the Other:

> *I now exist as myself for my unreflective consciousness...here the self comes to haunt the unreflective consciousness. (Sartre 1984, 348)*

The non-reflective consciousness, which objectifies the world, now apprehends itself as an object for another perceiving consciousness. Here, the situation of shame poignantly reveals the consciousness of the Other, not as a concept, but as an immediate subject. The Other's Look works its magic through the very essence and power of consciousness:

23

*The Other is present to me without any intermediary as a transcendence which is not mine...the being through whom I gain my objectness. (Sartre 1984, 361)*

Although we recognize a person by their physical qualities—the eyes, the mouth, sound, body—these are transcended by the consciousness of the Other:

*If I apprehend the look, I cease to perceive the eyes; they are there, they remain in the field of my perception as pure presentations...The Other's look hides his eyes; he seems to go in front of them. (Sartre 1984, 346)*

The perception of the Other, Sartre emphasizes, is a true subjectivity reaching across the physical world:

*The Other's look touches me across the world and is not only a transformation of myself but a total metamorphosis of the world. I am looked-at in a world which is looked-at. (Sartre 1984, 360)*

Although in his analysis Sartre depicts the emanation of the Other through shame, we encounter its transforming power as early as our infancy, with our parents. The newborn mind is pure non-reflective awareness. It is the attention and recognition, the Look, of parents that becomes the catalyst for the emergence of the infant's conscious point of view and for the development of the psychological Self. It is not by a fortuitus accident, or a fall from grace, that we arrive at Self-consciousness, but as the very means by which we become individual humans:

> *It would perhaps not be impossible to conceive of a For-itself which would be wholly free from all For-others and which would exist without even suspecting the possibility of being an object. But this For-itself would not be 'man.' What the cogito reveals to us here is just factual necessity: it is found--and this is indisputable--that our being along with its being-for-itself is also for-others; the being which is revealed to the reflective consciousness is for-itself-for-others. (Sartre 1984, 374-6)*

The interdependence of Self and Other underscores the importance of morality in our relationships. Because we are unable to observe ourselves, because we are an absolute subjectivity, we are dependent on the Other for our self-perception; we are at the mercy of the Other:

> *I cannot discover any truth whatsoever about myself except through the mediation of another. The other is essential to my existence, as well as to the knowledge I have of myself. (Sartre 2007, 41)*

The Other does not simply reflect the Me, it has the power to enslave Me. It harnesses this power from my Nothingness, from my lack of an inherent identity. This vulnerability is the source of the insecurity which is manipulated by sadists, dictators, cults, and gangs: "In so far as I am the object of values which come to qualify me without my being able to act on this qualification or even to know it, I am enslaved" (1984, 358).

This power to affect consciousness is critical in the developing child, whose mind is particularly susceptible and sensitive to the influence of others. The effect that parents and others have on young minds can be profound and life changing, especially in the early years when the mind is strongly receptive, malleable, and naive. The psychologist Mary Ainsworth developed a study, named *The Strange Situation,* to evaluate parent-infant bonding, where the reaction of young infants was observed after being left alone with a stranger and upon return of the parent (Ainsworth 1971). She found that the degree of acceptance of the stranger corresponded inversely to the degree of bonding with the parents and subsequent emotional stability of the child in later years. It has been well documented that the quality of life experienced throughout infancy and childhood has a significant impact on the development of the personality, emotional stability, and social involvement of a person, extending into adulthood (Siegel 1999).

The Other, being another Nothingness, is as much of a mystery to me as I am to myself. We apprehend each other across the body, but what transcends the body is the Nothingness. Although we easily recognize another self-consciousness, we are at loss to describe what it is we perceive. I can get lost in thought looking at a tree or a statue—it is not personal—but the Look of the Other reaches out and involves me. It has a power, a presence, a contingency. When we encounter another person there is always some kind of acknowledgement, some consequence, where even a disregard will entail mutual conscious effects. This is proof of a conscious presence, of a Being: that I cannot encounter another awareness without being affected in some way.

The interaction between the Self and Other is always complex. The more power we give the Other to assert our somethingness, the weaker and more vulnerable we become; less importance we give the other the more Nothing we become. Personal relationships generally involve this reciprocal power struggle: a press to keep from being overwhelmed or disintegrated.

The Buddha was very aware of the transformative power of human interactions. In his formulation of the Eightfold Path, he emphasized morality as one of the three main factors for achieving liberation (the other two being wisdom and meditation). The Buddha expressed the importance of this realization in his Metta Sutta:

*This is what should be done*
*By one who is skilled in goodness,*
*And who knows the path of peace: Let them be*
*able and upright,*
*Straightforward and gentle in speech,*
*Humble and not conceited,*
*Contented and easily satisfied,*
*Unburdened with duties and frugal in their ways.*
*Peaceful and calm and wise and skillful,*
*Not proud or demanding in nature.*
*Let them not do the slightest thing*
*That the wise would later reprove.*
*Wishing: In gladness and in safety,*
*May all beings be at ease...*
*Let none deceive another,*
*Or despise any being in any state.*
*Let none through anger or ill-will*
*Wish harm upon another.*
*Even as a mother protects with her life*
*Her child, her only child,*

28

*So with a boundless heart*
*Should one cherish all living beings;*
*Radiating kindness over the entire world...*
*Freed from hatred and ill-will*
*(Sn 1.8)*

## Freedom and the Unconditioned

We have seen that consciousness is as a Nothingness, a being which stands distinct from anything it can know yet knows itself in the act of knowing. Sartre arrives at the Nothingness through the investigation of negations:

> *Negation is an abrupt break in continuity which can not in any case result from prior affirmations; it is an original and irreducible event. Here we are in the realm of consciousness. Consciousness moreover cannot produce a negation except in the form of consciousness of negation...The not, as an abrupt intuitive discovery, appears as consciousness (of being), consciousness of the not. (Sartre 1984, 43)*

An absence of being cannot exist as a conscious experience of none-being because negations have no prior conditions; that is, we have no sense perception of something that does not exist. Thus, as Sartre explains, the naught must be intrinsic of the human consciousness: human being is a Being through whom non-being comes into the existence. From here Sartre asks: "What must man be in his being in order that through him nothingness may come to being?" (Sartre 1984, 59). In Being, humankind cannot be anything: it must Be without essence. And this means that in not being anything, Being must also exist as an absolute Freedom. It is because we are not anything, that we can be anything: "in establishing a certain conduct as a possibility, I am aware that "nothing" can compel me to adopt that conduct...nothing prevents me from precipitating myself into the abyss." (Sartre 1984, 69). This Freedom is not a concept, nor is it the pretense of an uninhibited self; but rather, it is an attribute of consciousness itself.

Evidence to this unconditioned freedom of the mind is the great divergence of human moral conduct: ranging from the most grandiose and humble sympathy to the most unfathomable cruelty. It is in fact because the human mind has no natural boundaries that a moral system is indispensable as a deterrent to the harm of self and others.

If human consciousness were constitutionally deterministic, then all behavior would be survival directed, and an unconsciousness:

*it is impossible to assign to a consciousness a motivation other than itself. Otherwise, it would be necessary to conceive that consciousness to the degree to which it is an effect, is not conscious (of) itself. It would be necessary in some manner that it should be without being conscious (of) being...But consciousness is consciousness through and through. (Sartre 1984, 15)*

Truly deterministic human beings would be like complex ants or bees. In contrast, human consciousness is the seat of unbound creativity, inspiration, and conflict.

Sartre discerned the Freedom of Nothingness through rigorous philosophical analysis, yet this Freedom can be experienced directly with meditation. In deep meditation, a practitioner can release all the objects of consciousness and abide in unconditioned mind. This can be experienced as well in daily life with the practice of mindfulness. When you develop the ability to be alert to the subtle movements of the mind, you learn to refrain from reacting to enticements, and your awareness can remain in a peaceful state despite intense internal or external distractions.

When the mind has created a psychological distance from the World, and it is centered on itself, then there is true freedom; in this there is no becoming, there is a sense of stillness. The mind becomes like a mountain, unaffected by even the worst weather.

The untrained mind is pulled and enthralled by the objects of the world. It *merges* with the things of the world to the extent that the mind *becomes* its objects. It is in this sense that the ordinary mind is bound to and conditioned by its own conscious perceptions. For the ordinary unenlightened person, there is no free will. Sartre calls this the "serious man," the one who is bound by the very values she/he creates. Unless one learns to objectify, observe, and transcend the khandhas, one will be subject to them as a Self. The unobserved mind is a slave to habits, instincts, and emotions, and a victim to the will of the Others.

In a profound and obscure way, we are afraid of our freedom. We are afraid of losing control because there is nothing controlling us, nothing to hold on to. And we fear the responsibility and consequences of unconditioned freedom. Thus, we reach for a sense of meaning, create values, search for something to grab onto to keep us from wavering. Seeking identity, we become a family member, a church member, a student, a professional, or a non-conformist, a sinner, a saint. Yet, to live in ignorance of the true nature of the Self is to live a victim of our own creations and those of our predecessors. The "serious man" lives in dread of his values: all safe in a gilded cage.

Buddhism shows the way to the freedom of the unconditioned mind. However, deliverance takes courage. It means facing the truth, the unfamiliar, the strange. In the early stages of realization, when the World begins to fall away, when body is simply flesh and bones, and the thoughts and emotions as phantasms, there is a feeling of disorientation, an existential nausea, as the minds struggles to find footing in the Nothingness. All that was familiar and normal and reasonable is transformed into relative and abstract. But, for those who endure in the Nothingness of Not-self, there is the reward of an authentic happiness and true freedom of mind. There, at the center of all that changes is the "One Who Knows," the unchanging, the fearless: The emancipated Being.

# From Bad Faith to Nibbana

C "consciousness is a being, the nature of which is to be conscious of the nothingness of its being," declared Sartre regarding the essence of human existence. This perduring condition of not knowing who we are, this ominous Nothingness confronting us as anguish or unnerving boredom, becomes the impetus for the creation of a Self, to exist as something in the world. However, as Gautama the Buddha observed, since everything that we can experience is impermanent, we can never formulate a self-image which is lasting or accurate but only a wavering and distorted reflection that is subject to change and temporality. This Self, we hold in Bad Faith.

In his analysis of Bad Faith, Sartre describes a cafe waiter who appears too theatrical in the performance of his job:

> *his movement is quick and forward, a little too precise, a little too rapid...trying to imitate in his walk*

> *the inflexible stiffness of some kind of automa-*
> *ton...carrying his tray with the recklessness of a tight-*
> *rope-walker...he is playing at being a waiter in a café.*
> *(Sartre 1984, 101)*

He points out that this waiter is acting out his idea of what it is like to be a cafe waiter. He is trying to become something which he can never fully realize, since all his attempts will ultimately disintegrate into his Nothingness.

Human being in the world is always a creation, always a becoming. There are many roles which we play in our daily lives in response to situations we encounter. These are learned ways of behaving which we have adopted from our culture and family. If you attend carefully to your mind, you can note how these self-creations appear and change in your daily activities and encounters with others. These various roles are fused into a vague idea of Me. As Shakespeare wisely expressed in his play, *As You Like It,* we are actors:

> *All the world's a stage,*
> *And all the men and women merely players;*
> *They have their exits and their entrances,*
> *And one man in his time plays many parts*

We create our personalities and create the life we live and believe it to be our reality.

This conviction that we are something solid, authentic, in the world Sartre calls Bad Faith. However, the waiter is not in Bad Faith because he is pretending to be something he is not. He is in Bad Faith because he is forsaking his true nature as Nothingness and forgoing the freedom which it affords: "The goal of bad faith, as we said, is to put oneself out of reach; it is an escape" (Sartre 1984, 110). Bad Faith is an attempt to escape the anguish and emptiness of non-being by creating a Self-perception. We attempt to escape the Nothingness by placing our faith on a Self which is not real, believing it our essence. It is a false faith. In doing this, we renounce our essential freedom, and our opportunity to be true to ourselves, to be authentic. Sartre did not see an escape from Bad Faith, however, as any attempt at pure sincerity, at authenticity, would result in just another Self project. Consciousness, he felt, is doomed to not be what it is, and to be what it is not.

In his plan at a remedy for human psychological suffering, the Buddha aimed his therapy at the source: desire. We suffer because of our ignorance as to the true nature of existence; because we desire a world which is constantly changing, impermanent, and thus can never be fulfilling. Desire is an intention. It is the movement of the mind towards an object deemed as valuable. Desire is

Karma. Karma is an intention which conditions cause and effect, or the consequences of actions. Then thirst (a necessity of water) becomes a desire for a beer, or a frustration when there is nothing to drink. The suffering caused by desire is reflective; it is psychological. One can feel pain, but it becomes suffering when we do not want it or feel we do not deserve it. And even when a desire is satisfied, we suffer the fear of loss. The psychological pain that is caused by the frustration of a craving is remarkable. Even a young child, when denied an object of desire, will react with an expression of pain comparable to significant physical injury. The mental pain from the loss of a loved one can be torturous. Desire is a movement of the Self.

From an existential point of view, however, we find that the motivation behind desire originates deeper than just a selfish urge, but rather, from a *Lack* at the heart of being:

> *The existence of desire as a human fact is sufficient to prove that human reality is a lack...desire is a lack of being...it is this for-itself which we have apprehended as not being what it is and being what it is not. (Sartre 1984, 137)*

Desire is not the disease, but a symptom of a more pernicious condition: the fear of non-being. It is the desire to escape from the Nothingness which engenders the project of Self. Desire is the psychological strategy by which we attempt to escape our No-thingness, to satiate our emptiness with the things of the world. Psychological suffering originates, not so much from the craving of an impermanent world, but from the ever-nagging, visceral dread of non-existence, of being nothing. It is this subconscious fear of the Nothingness which drives our perilous journey into the World; a journey marked by suffering and confusion, by Bad Faith. This is the truth behind our misguided intentions, acts of cruelty, and most profound fears. This is the truth we need to face to find peace of mind, wholesomeness, and integrity.

In the practice of Buddhism, when the desire for the World falls away as Not-self an existential void is created: This is the Nothingness, an existential dark night. At first the practitioner rejoices in the newfound freedom rendered by the release of Self-identity. But soon this freedom opens to a foundation in Nothing, and the aspirant becomes as a stranger in a strange land. Seeing oneself an emptiness, a suchness, in a world of relativities, the practitioner subconsciously longs for a return to the Self, which has now become an alien entity. This emptiness at the heart of being cannot be satisfied but by a consummation in Being. If this Being is forsaken, as by a No-self doctrine, then a

39

suppressed longing for the Self continues to burn, precipitating a surrender to indifference, or purposelessness, or emotional crisis.

In his book, *After the Ecstasy, the Laundry,* Jack Kornfield relates numerous accounts from meditation practitioners who after experiencing enlightenment soon became disenchanted and depressed. Their stories reveal a regular pattern of intense and protracted struggle with aspects of the ego; followed by a sudden dissolution of the Self, associated with intense feelings of joy, mental release, and a sense of freedom, lasting a few weeks; then developing frustration with mundane life, personal conflicts, and symptoms of depression. What they experienced was an existential crisis brought about by faith in a No-self doctrine, a catapult to existential Emptiness.

The Buddha's therapy for the end of suffering is directed at eliminating the desire for the world as Self. He taught that the things of the world, the khandhas, are a source of suffering because they are impermanent, and therefore not satisfying and Not-(a true)-self. The Khandhas cannot be eliminated for they are the World we live in, but once their true nature is comprehended, the fascination for them is cooled, and the delusion of the Self is released.

What is difficult is the realization of what is left after the Self is released. To be rigorous, the Buddha could not describe what remains after Enlightenment without generating another Self, another idea of self. When pointing at this with the concepts as No-mind, Original mind, Absolute Subjectivity, or Being, we still run the risk of fomenting more confusion, of making it something which we are not and have to become. Therefore, in his great wisdom, the Buddha left the source of the Self unconditioned, as Not-self, to establish a straight path to realization. Once everything is released as Not-self, then the true essence of existence is spontaneously revealed:

> *Bhikkhus, when a noble follower who has heard (the truth) sees thus, he finds estrangement in form, he finds estrangement in feeling, he finds estrangement in perception, he finds estrangement in determinations, he finds estrangement in consciousness.*
>
> *When he finds estrangement, passion fades out. With the fading of passion, he is liberated. (SN 22.59) (Access to Insight. 2010)*

For this very reason, the interpretation of the Anatta-lakkhana Sutta— (SN 22.59) (Access to Insight. 2010)—as a No-self doctrine leads to an immediate dead end, to unreconcilable absurdity, to Nothing.

Desire is cooled through acceptance; what Buddhis teacher Ajahn Sumedho calls "the way it is" (Sumedho 1989). Acceptance is the way of letting go. It is a pre-reflective *knowing* of the world as other, as Not-self, and thereof not creating a desire for it, nor a resistance to it. When the mind does not reach for anything, it remains centered. For, if there is no desire, there is no lacking. Since the World is impermanent, all that is necessary to arrive at Enlightenment is wisdom, patience, and acceptance.

Acceptance, however, is not indifference. It rather engages the world-as-it-is with the wholesome intent; everything is approached and managed with the wisdom (clear comprehension) and equanimity as to what is most appropriate and beneficial for oneself and others.

The best method for developing Acceptance is with the practice of mindfulness and concentration meditation. Concentration meditation is achieved by sitting quietly and apprehending everything which appears to the mind as being an object of consciousness. This creates a space for the mind to know itself as not being any of its objects. With mindfulness one develops the ability to establish objectiveness while functioning in the world.

When the awareness of Being, as Not-self, is fully realized, then there is nothing in the world that reflects a self-image, nothing that pulls self-consciousness into the World. Consciousness (awareness) is then like a wind with nothing to move:

> *If a monk abandons passion for the property of form... feeling... perception... fabrications... consciousness, then owing to the abandonment of passion, the support is cut off, and there is no base for consciousness. Consciousness, thus unestablished, not proliferating, not performing any function, is released. Owing to its release, it is steady. Owing to its steadiness, it is contented. Owing to its contentment, it is not agitated. Not agitated, he (the monk) is totally unbound right within. (SN 22.53) (Bhikkhu 2005)*

What could be referred to as the true self, as that which knows the world as Not-self, cannot be objectively appreciated, but it is not lacking in intrinsic qualities. This essential Being is a certitude of existing. When emancipated, as Not-self, since unbound from all things, it is experienced as a lightness of awareness. It requires no energy to be aware. In contrast, thinking requires energy, concentration, and it feels forceful and heavy to the mind. Unlike the nouns No-Mind and Original Mind, Being (as a present participle) is not something that we can think about; it is all action; it is existing; and it is something that we can realize as an experience with meditation.

The natural state of Being is inevitably wholesome and peaceful. The Buddha referred to the four *Brahma-viharas* as the sublime attributes, which manifest once the illusion of the Self is lifted, namely: loving-kindness *(metta)*, compassion *(karuna)*, empathy *(mudita),* and equanimity *(upekka)*. Authentic Being is spontaneous: It is noble, courageous, truthful, righteous, self-effacing, self-sacrificing

Authenticity cannot refer to a Self or any form of conceptual being. It is a manifestation of the non-reflective consciousness as emancipated Being. Without the methodology of Buddhism, it is exceedingly difficult to transcend Bad Faith towards authentic Being—it would require a radical dissolution of the Self, such as resulting from severe depression or a severe traumatic experience, and then a re-founding of the non-reflective consciousness as unconditioned Being. Authentic Being is the culmination of Unbinding, or Nibbana (Nirvana).

Nibbana is emancipated Being. When Gautama the Buddha pointed to the *nameless*, he did not point an emptiness or absence, but instead, to positive qualities, to a Fullness of Existence:

*the true, the beyond, the subtle, the very-hard-to-see, the ageless, permanence, the undecaying, the surfaceless, non-objectification, peace, the deathless, the exquisite, bliss, solace, the exhaustion of craving, the wonderful, the marvelous, the secure, security, nibbāna, the unafflicted, the passionless, the pure, release, non-attachment, the island, shelter, harbor, refuge, the ultimate. (SN 42.1-44) (Bhikkhu 1999)*

# Facticity and Kamma

Kamma (or karma in Sanskrit) can be simply defined as the law of cause and effect. Yet kamma is not simple, and it is a burdensome condition of our existence. Most of us are as unaware of our contingency as of our Nothingness. This ignorance robs us of peace of mind and happiness and engenders hostility, discrimination, abuse, and wars. We think we are in control, but we are often ingenuous victims of our own intentions. Kamma is what Sartre calls Facticity:

> *The for-itself is, in so far as it appears in a condition which it has not chosen. . . it is in so far as it is thrown into a world and abandoned in a "situation"; it is as pure contingency inasmuch as for it as for things in the world . . . It is in so far as there is in it something of which it is not the foundation. (Sartre 1984,127)*

We are heirs to the contingency of the universe. We are, at the present time, the effects of causes upon causes leading back to the beginning of time, to the Big Bang. We, the thinking beings, are the offspring of the universe, the latest and the greatest. Elements formed from the explosions of stars combined to form the minerals of the earth, which in turn interacted to form molecules, which, after many eons of evolution, have come to constitute our present bodies.

Born as a body, and developing in it, we become accustomed to it and identify it as who we are. We wash it, dress it, odorize it. We measure ourselves and others by its length, weight, and splendor. And yet, we are aware of only a small portion of our physical makeup. If you sit still, with eyes closed, and draw your attention to your body, you may notice that which contacts your skin, the pressure of the weight of the body, some pain you may have, or perhaps at itch. You will not notice the constant and dynamic beating of the heart, 70 times per minute, nor the circulation of the blood to the cells of the body. We are not conscious of our kidneys constantly filtrating gallons of blood daily to produce urine and maintaining the blood pressure and the concentration of minerals in the blood to decimals of a difference. Not aware of the liver performing hundreds of chemical reactions that regulate the digestion and detoxify the blood. We are unaware of the movement and absorption of nutrients throughout our 25 feet of intestines. We are insensible to most of our organs and ignorant to the vast complexities which take place for our bodies to survive another day. Moreover, if one of your kidneys were removed and placed next to that of another person your age, you would not be able to identify your own. Similarly, if someone were to claim "this is my home" but could not describe what furniture was in the living room, the color of the walls, or how many bedrooms it has, then we could comfortably conclude that it was not their home. Although we are sentient of our bodies and its pains, we have little knowledge or control of it. The reality of the body is that it conforms more to the forces of nature than to our will— "for dust thou art and unto dust shall thou return" (Genesis 3:19). The body is Not-self.

The kamma of the body happens to us. This is most easily seen with reproduction. As the urge for existence, sex is the most primitive of energies, which constrains to create life even in the most unfavorable of conditions. It is the fuel of evolution. We experience the sexual drive as if we own it, as if it were our idea, yet it drives even very educated minds to violate the strongest prohibitions, to risk everything for brief encounter. Sex is stressful. Its energy takes over the mind with powerful emotions and irrational motivations, and it mesmerizes

48

our perceptions and common sense. In other words, sex happens to us. And it is typically brief and impermanent.

Sartre further demonstrates that the body, which we believe we know, is in effect given to us by the Other: it is a concept. We are informed of our attractiveness, or lack thereof, by other persons, as we lack perspective to our bodies. The physical body is "lived and not known," Sartre says. Consciousness rather transcends the body in its intentions: "I do not apprehend my hand in the act of writing but only the pen which is writing. . . I am my hand. . . the body is present in every action although invisible" (Sartre 1984, 426-27).

Although the body is Not-self, it is not simply a container for consciousness, not an avatar, but the means by which consciousness comes to individual Being. It is the template for forging of an individual autonomous existence:

> *This inapprehensible body is precisely the necessity that there be a choice, that I do not exist all at once. In this sense my finitude is the condition of my freedom, for there is no freedom without choice; and in the same way that the body conditions consciousness as pure consciousness of the world, it renders consciousness possible even in its very freedom. (Sartre 1984, 432)*

We are the product of conditions emanating from our psychological, physical, familial, social, cultural, genetic, environmental, and evolutional heritage. So then, are we destined to remain slaves to our contingency, of our Karma? The Buddha did not think so, and he expressed this in is powerful Not-self doctrine.

We are victims of our own creation, of our attachment to the idea of Self. The psychological energy of the anger, for example, is strongly modulated by the fixation on Self. Anger is the natural, evolutionary reaction to a threat of injury. Primitive animals and humans increased their physical and psychological energy to fend against powerful aggressors by secreting adrenalin, triggered by the instinctive emotion of anger. As modern humans, we do the same when threatened with injury; however, what we are fighting against most of the time is our own mind.

The reaction of anger involves the function of the amygdala (an almond sized structure in the limbic system of the brain) that affects the energy of the body through neuronal and hormonal systems. We use the limbic system and the amygdala in the same manner we use the motor center in the brain to move our legs. It is not the amygdala that perceives a dangerous situation and then sends signals to the cortex, as some researchers suggest, but rather the aggressive situation is first rapidly apprehended by the non-reflective consciousness (the awareness), which then stimulates the amygdala to trigger the release of hormones, and then the situation is reflected upon by rational (reflective) cortex of the brain. The amygdala is a modulating organ, not a thinking one; it is a relay center. If the amygdala were removed then a threat would be perceived but there would be no mechanism for an emotional reaction, in the same manner that you cannot run if you cannot control your legs.

The reaction of anger is modulated by a complex mechanism of instincts and reflection. We are no longer fighting saber tooth tigers, but when someone insults us, we react with the same emotional energy. We defend our ego, our self-integrity, against the aggressions of the world with the release of catecholamines that are triggered by anger. Even after the threat is gone, long after the argument has ended, we continue to fight our belligerent thoughts with our nervous system and hormones, which if persistent can lead to stress, anxiety, high blood pressure, and even immune disfunction.

Because we are a Nothingness, we become our intentions and actions as that is all we see, all that we can palpate. We grasp the anger that is generated by the circumstances of the world as our anger. We become the anger (the criticism, the envy, the jealousy) we direct at others—as well as the love and affection we treat others with. We become the emotions because we believe they are our Self. But as we have seen, the emotions, like sex, are things that happen to us; things that we can see as at a distance from our point of view as objects of our consciousness.

The Buddha designed the Eightfold Path for the purpose of liberating the mind from the attachment to Self, for liberating the mind from the influence of Karma. If all we are is an illusion of Self, if there is nothing other than the Self, then there would be no escape, no liberation, from the grip of Karma, from Facticity.

Karma, or Facticity, result from becoming. We become our intentions and our actions because we are a Nothingness trying to be a Somethingness. Karma and facticity are the result of believing in a Self. When we release the Self, we are no longer psychologically subject to Karma, only to the conditions intrinsic of physical existence: This is the end of suffering; this is Unbinding.

Understanding of the law of cause and effect, or karma, is an integral part for developing the wisdom which, combined with meditation and morality, lead to liberation of consciousness from attachment to the Self. Clear understanding of the Not-self doctrine is imperative to attaining our freedom from conditioning.

# Consciousness and the Self

T he origin of consciousness disappears into
the Nothingness. Like a spotlight glowing
from out of nowhere, the mind seems to appear
only in reflecting the world:

> *The knower is not; he is not apprehensible. He is*
> *nothing other than that which brings it about that*
> *there is being-there on the part of the known, a pres-*
> *ence . . . the presence appears then across the total*
> *translucency of the knower known, an absolute pres-*
> *ence. (Sartre 1984, 246)*

As we have already determined, self-consciousness cannot originate from the objects of consciousness, from thoughts, because then it would
be an un-self-consciousness, as there would be no
awareness connecting one thought to another. But
if everything that we can be conscious of are the

objects of consciousness (i.e., thoughts, and sense perceptions), then how do we know we exist? How is it that we experience self-existence?

"The knower is not apprehensible," concluded Sartre, but this is as an object of reflection, from reasoning. However, with meditation, another point of view is revealed.

With deep concentration meditation, a practitioner can focus on the breathing until no thoughts or bodily perceptions appear to the mind. Eventually, the perception of breathing itself fades away, and one is left only aware of being aware: an awareness of awareness. This is like aiming a spotlight into a clear dark night: no objects are revealed even though there is a light shining. It is an experience of pure awareness. After some practice, this awareness of existing can be experienced outside of meditation. Although some practitioners describe it as the space in a room rather than the furniture, this experience is not accessible to thinking. It is a purely subjective experience, and therefore, it cannot be elucidated with words. It is the reason the Buddha pointed to this reality as Not-self, and I indicate it with Being (as the present participle).

Now, if I were to ask you "how do you know you exist," you would think it the most obvious question but the most difficult to answer. If you answer, "I think, therefore, I am," the awareness of thinking comes first; it is rather "I am, therefore, I think." But even still, this would be an experience of thinking and not of existing, not of being. It is difficult to be aware of your existence because it *is* where everything *is*. But if you are certain of anything, it is that you exist. That certitude of existence, that sense of presence, is the experience of being self-conscious: the experience of Being. You know that you exist because you know that you exist.

Martin Heidegger went to great lengths to explain this experience of Being, but few have been able to fully grasp his profound insight—probably not even Sartre.

The awareness of Being is the aim of the Not-self doctrine. With the realization of not being the Self, the mind is released from the cause of suffering: the very attachment to Self. For it is the desire of the World as Self which brings about anger, fear, frustration, sadness, and all other psychological suffering. Even with the joy of getting what you want, there is always the fear of possible loss.

It is because Being is a Nothingness, an absolute subjectivity, that the World it reflects on is an Emptiness. Since everything which is experienced is an object of consciousness (since the world itself cannot be directly experienced), then everything is of the essence of the Nothingness of consciousness. Simply said, everything is made of consciousness. What this Being, this Nothingness, this Emptiness is, is the unfathomable mystery of existence: it is what it is. Therefore, all is Emptiness and Emptiness is all (The Heart Sutra). Being is Emptiness; and Emptiness is a fullness of Being.

The great error in understanding Buddhism is the belief that self-consciousness is the Self: the conception of the self-conscious experience as a phenomenon: The misapprehension of the knower. This fallacy is well illustrated in the following redaction of a well-known dialogue between King Melinda and the monk Nagasena, around 150 BCE, regarding the nature of the Self:

> *King Melinda and Thera Nagasena, the latter wishing to explain to the King this law of aggregates, enquired from the King how he came there, whether on foot or riding. The King replied that he came in a chariot.*
>
> *"Your Majesty," said Nagasena, "if you came in a chariot, declare to me the chariot. Is the pole the chariot?" "Truly not," said the King. "Is the axle the chariot," asked Nagasena. "Truly not," said the King. "Is the chariot-body the chariot?" — "Truly not," said the King. "Is the yoke the chariot?" —*

*"Truly not," said the King. "Are the reins the chariot?" — "Truly not," said the King. "Is the goading stick the chariot?" — "Truly not," said the King. "Where then, Oh King," asked Nagasena, "is this chariot in which you say you came?"*

*Similarly, "human being," "man," "I" are mere names and terms, not corresponding to anything that is really and actually existing. In the ultimate sense there exist only changing energies. . .*

*Thoughts arise, one following the other with such a rapidity of succession that the illusion of a permanent thing called "the mind" is created; but really there is no permanent thing but only a flow of thoughts. The rapid succession of thoughts is compared to the flow of water in a river, one drop following another in rapid succession that we seem to see a permanent entity in this flow. But this is an illusion. Similarly, there is no such permanent entity as the mind. It is only a succession of thoughts, a stream of thoughts that arise and pass away. . .*

*When analysis reveals that there is no person but only a process, that there is no doer but only a deed, we arrive at the conclusion that there is no person who dies, but that there is only a process of dying. Moving is a process, walking is a process, so dying is also a process. Just as there is no hidden agent back and behind the process of moving or walking, so,*

*there is no hidden agent back and behind the process*
*of dying. (Gunaratna 1982)*

Here, the observer of the chariot, as well as the observer of the thoughts, is overlooked. The question is: Which thought is it that knows that there is a flow of thoughts? The good monk overlooks the One who knows that there are thoughts—or that there is a chariot. It is like someone coming out of a room and asserting that there was no one there, that the room was empty. It is like saying "I do not exist." The comparison with the chariot makes sense only logically, but it is describing something which cannot be experienced: thoughts without a Thinker. This is the problem with logic, that you can make a logical representation of a reality that is not real.

If consciousness were one of the aggregates, then there would have to exist another consciousness which is aware of the impermanence of the aggregate of consciousness—that sees the flow of thoughts, or the flow of water. The statement "consciousness is not self" of the Not-self doctrine means that the consciousness of the world, the consciousness of objects, is not the One who knows, not the non-reflective consciousness. The Not-self doctrine rightly points at the chariot rider, to the Knower. What is not real, what is made of parts, with no actual entity, is the Self.

To argue that there is no real entity, no individual, no person who is aware of their existence, but only an amalgam of conditions, is not profound. It is what science says: that there are only molecules, energies, evolution, and reproducing genes. It makes an illusion of all that is most human: morality, justice, aesthetics, creativity, charity, sympathy, and Being. The truth is, that if there is no individual being, no human Being, then all values and ideals, all purpose and ambition, are illusions as well, and then there is truly nothing.

If consciousness were not an unconditioned subjectivity, if it were the objects of consciousness, then objective observations would not be possible since awareness would be limited to the perception, the mind moment; it would be an un-self-consciousness. If consciousness were not unconditioned, then it would be impossible to do concentration meditation.

Emptiness already implies a fullness, as Not-self already implies an observing self: The Knower.

## The Fourth Ekstasis and Enlightenment

I n what Sartre calls a First Ekstasis, consciousness accomplishes existential awareness
through a nihilation of being In-itself from itself,
hence becoming a Nothingness in consummating
being For-itself. This Sartre explains is solely a human process by which consciousness becomes
self-conscious. In a Second Ekstasis, self-consciousness, constrained by its Nothingness, exerts
itself to grasp the world in the form of a Self: to
clothe itself with the physical, to become something. As a Third Ekstasis, self-awareness consoli-
dates an objective existence in acknowledging itself an object for the consciousness of the Other,
"a fall through an absolute emptiness toward ob-
jectivity" (Sartre 1984, 367).

With Buddhism the possibility of a Fourth Ekstasis arises, as consciousness, in apprehending the
World as stressful and Not-self, transcends it towards a new freedom:

*And yet when the mind is empty, the senses are still all right. It's not like being in a trance, totally oblivious to everything; your mind is open, empty--or you might call it whole, complete, bright.... But the beautiful objects and the ugly ones are all in the space and to notice space you withdraw your attention from the objects of beauty and ugliness. (Ajahn Sumedho 1989)*

The catalyst for this further maturation is the sudden awareness of the inherent freedom of non-reflective being, enabling an emancipation from the World:

*Freedom is precisely the nothingness which is made-to-be at the heart of man...Thus freedom is not a being; it is the being of man - i.e., his nothingness of being. (Sartre 1984,569)*

The spiritual teacher Eckhart Tolle recounts how he woke up one night with "absolute dread." He had been suffering more many years from chronic anxiety and attacks of suicidal depression, but this one night it was especially intense with a "deep longing for annihilation, for nonexistence." As he thought, "I cannot live with myself any longer," he realized that there was a thought and a thinker of the thought. His mind felt then as if it had been "sucked into a void" and suddenly all his fears were gone. He spent the following 5 months in silent joyful peace (Tolle 1999, 3-4). This transformative experience is analogous to what is called Enlightenment in Buddhism. This sudden freeing of the mind is also described by practitioners of Zen as Satori. Zen involves a process of frustrating the rational mind to the point where the awareness releases it. Enlightenment is the sudden realization that the awareness is not the Self, the realization of the absolute Freedom of consciousness.

Gautama the Buddha most likely had a similar enlightenment experience, albeit much more penetrating. He had been living for several years as an ascetic, practicing heroic acts of extreme abstinence and meditation, which at times brought him dangerously close to death. Then one day he realized that what he was doing was not working. So, he ate well and sat resolute in meditation under a fig tree, the Bodhi tree, and arose the following day with the Enlightenment that led to his formulation of the Eightfold Path to Nibbana.

Being is existence. It is a certainty of existence. It is what it feels as "here and now." It is the source of our humanness. Being cannot be thought of or understood or felt, as it is not an object of the mind: It is the mind. It is where everything exists. It is the source of our humanity: of our sense of beauty, justice, sympathy, kindness, and love.

Enlightenment is the emancipation of Being from the World-as-Self. After this first release, however, it takes insight and time for the non-reflective consciousness to fully assert its autonomy. Gautama had already disciplined his mind through meditation and mindfulness for many years and possessed a brilliant intellect, all that made his transcendence a most profound and unique experience. Once the individual has realized (not just understood) this absolute Freedom of the mind, then the development of Mindfulness and Wisdom can execute the radical release of the Self. The complete emancipation of Being from the World-as-Self is Unbinding, or Nibbana (Nirvana in Sanskrit).

The fully Enlightened Being is peaceful. The Empty Mind, the Liberated Mind, the Being-in-itself, is ethereal and effortless. It is all-encompassing yet transparent. Not contingent on anything, it is confident, fearless, selfless.

Enlightenment and Unbinding are a maturing. It is the attainment of the greatest human potential.

# Being and Beethoven

It is perplexing how a music of such coherence, beauty, and restrained elegance could have originated from a man of such gross personal attributes as Ludwig Van Beethoven. He distinguished himself from his Viennese patrons and admirers by his coarse manners and speech: "His movements were awkward and clumsy, and he constantly overturned or broke things" (Lockwood 2003, 78). He was rude, vulgar, condescending, and easily angered. His hair and clothes as unkempt as his home. Yet, his music is grandiose, elegant, and oftentimes transcendental.

He was born into a working-class family of Bonn, the second child to an abused mother and alcoholic father, and as a result, suffered much in his youth. Bernhard Maurer, a friend of the Beethoven family, reports that the child Beethoven "outside of music understood nothing of social life;

consequently, he was ill-humored with other people, did not know how to converse with them, and withdrew into himself." Mr. Maurer as well noted that the elder Beethoven, often, after his tavern rounds, would awaken young Ludwig and make him practice the piano till morning. His treatment of the young Beethoven was described as frequently violent and cruel (Solomon 1998, 22-26).

During his late twenties to early thirties (1797 to 1801), Beethoven suffered greatly from chronic diarrhea and the gradual loss of hearing to both ears. He was also often grieved from deep romantic attachments, with many love overtures but few reciprocated. Yet despite being severely depressed and borderline suicidal, it was during this time that he produced many extraordinary musical compositions, in almost all genres: "I live entirely in my music," he wrote to a friend (Solomon 1998, 149).

The great mystery of music hinges on the great mystery of consciousness. It is the pre-reflective consciousness, as Being, which gives meaning and beauty to the juxtaposition of sounds which we appreciate as music. While the allure of popular song is derived mostly from an organic response to rhythm and climax, with classical music rhythm and climax are subdued, and the appeal emerges instead from an intangible quality which seems as if drawn out from the Nothingness, as something

wondrous which we are pressed to describe. Composers frequently ascribe the source of their inspiration as coming from a place beyond the personal,
often unable to put into words the meaning of
their composition (Lockwood 2003, 15-21). This
mysterious, transpersonal quality is conspicuous in
all master works of art. It is also remarkable that
many great composers not only produced master-
pieces while suffering from significant physical or
psychological illness, but that they also seemed to
be inspired by their affliction. Perhaps it is the illness that induces the release of Being from the
constraints of the Self, allowing for greater creative
flow.

The Fifth Symphony begins with pounding
angst. It was composed between 1804 to 1808, after Beethoven had lost most of his hearing and was
suffering from loud ringing of the ears. The first
movement is a projection of existential anguish in
the face of a disintegrating Self. The anxious
pounding of the first theme, in the scale C minor
(the scale of despair), is overwhelming throughout.
This is the Being (the will to live) of Beethoven
fighting against a fragile and failing Self, wrestling
with the absurdity of a deaf musician.

The fourth movement, however, unfolds gloriously and triumphant with a life-affirming heroic
Yes! It is this expression of transcendence, which

beyond its structure and creativity, gives this composition its enduring and moving power.

Transcendence and magnificence are palpable of all masterworks of art. Yet art is superfluous. Since the creation of art offers no survival benefit, it would seem from this perspective a waste of time and energy. Nevertheless, art is universal of human existence. The Paleolithic cave paintings of 40 thousand years ago already demonstrate a celebration of the transcendent power of consciousness: an affirmation of human awareness.

Sartre considered humankind a being whose being is in question, which is tantamount saying that humankind is a being in search of meaning. What we learn from Beethoven and a myriad of other artists is that the meaning of Being is like the meaning of Art: it is in-itself meaningful. Art reflects the inherent meaningfulness of Being. In other words, it is Being which gives meaning to the World, which makes everything worthwhile. The absolutely subjective Being is absolutely meaningful and the source of all values. Our perception of inherent meaning, like our pre-reflective self-consciousness, is so immanent of our awareness, that it goes largely undetected. We project meaning unto the World but then unwittingly suffer to find it. Or to put it another way, human Being is as much suspended in Meaning as in Nothingness.

What should be most natural for a deterministic being is to be totally unconcerned with self-existence and meaning: to just exist. That religious expression and existential angst are ubiquitous to human existence should not be mistaken as ignorance or naivete, but rather as a quest to find meaning in a meaningless World. What is truly naive is to believe that human existence could derive any real sustenance from relative values.

Human meaningfulness is crystallized in our works of art, yet the greatest work of art is the human itself. Each individual person is a wondrous aesthetic expression of the physical and the conscious. Even the simplest person reveals a most profound drama of living: with love, hate, suffering, longing, care. Each person, despite appearing miniscule in relation to the cosmos, is a conscious window to the universe, a conscious singularity.

# Conclusion

T he essence of human consciousness is all at
once Not-self, Nothingness, and Being.
From the perspective of reflection, as the origin of
negation and the antithesis of everything that can
be thought of to exist, it is as nothing, a Nothingness; it is, as Sartre noted, at a conceptual distance
from the World. From an empirical perspective, as
it cannot take itself as an object of awareness, it is
an absolute subjectivity, and therefore, can only
clearly indicated as Not-self. As self-awareness and
the awareness of everything that exists, it is as a
fullness of Being.

From the point of view of Being, the practice
and principles of Buddhism are coherent and co-
gent. Everything that we can observe, that we are
conscious of, is not what we are, is not our Being:
it is Not-self. The observer must necessarily be
outside of what is observed, or known, and cannot
know itself. What we are is Being: knowing, willing,

existing. Yet even to state this is inaccurate, it is just another designation, another distorted reflection. The Self which we create to abide in the world, to interact with each other, is impermanent, and a source of stress and suffering: if we identify with it, and if we take it as our being. The Self and the World are Empty of inherent Being.

Our Nothingness is the reflection (our conceptualization) of Being in the world. From the point of view of reason, we are an existence without essence. When centered in Being, after having released the World-as-self, we are a Fullness, an actuality. In Being, we are innately Free; we are unconditioned. We enslave ourselves through ignorance when we limit ourselves by grasping the world as Self.

Being is a certitude of existing; it is a here and now awareness of existing. It cannot be revealed by argument nor representation, for, as Sartre indicated, it is a "pre-reflective Cogito." Being is the ground of all knowing. It is what makes everything real. The realization of unconditioned Being is the basis for psychological liberation.

The surest way up the mountain to Liberation is the Eightfold Path. Gautama the Buddha worked it out to perfection. The path, the cure of suffering, is straight forward and simple, as any authentic truth should be; we only make it complicated by thinking about it too much. There is nothing to acquire, nothing that we need, but just things to let go of on the path to Unbinding. Ultimately, when the fire of attachment to the Self has cooled, there are no heavenly trumpets or mystical lights, no otherworldly revelations, or special powers, but just our ordinary mind, clear, peaceful, uninhibited, comprehending, just a being there.

The interpretation of *anatta* as "empty of an entity" is a theoretical construct, and not something that can be experienced as such. It is tantamount to claiming you are blind while seeing things. Like saying "I don't exist." The doctrine of Not-self does not require a theory of Non-being for it to work.

The error lies in interpreting the Not-self doctrine as a metaphysical proposition. The Not-self doctrine is a pragmatic formulation, unique and fundamental to the understanding and practice of Buddhism. Gautama the Buddha saw the problem of human suffering as an urgent condition. Therefore, he did not concern himself and others with metaphysical questions, but, as a good physician, he formulated the best cure for the ailment—he wanted to remove the arrow of suffering before the patient died. The way to Nibbana, to Unbinding, is straightforward as declared by Gautama the Buddha:

> *And what is declared by me? 'This is stress,' is declared by me. 'This is the origination of stress,' is declared by me. 'This is the cessation of stress,' is declared by me. 'This is the path of practice leading to the cessation of stress,' is declared by me. And why are they declared by me? Because they are connected with the goal, are fundamental to the holy life. They lead to disenchantment, to dispassion, to cessation, to calm, to direct knowledge, to self-awakening, to unbinding. That's why they are declared by me. (Bhikkhu 2011)*

There is always a perceiver, always a conscious point of view. There is something that perceives the Self as an illusion, and that perceiver cannot be the illusion itself. With the Not-self doctrine, the Buddha is pointing at the source of all knowing, which cannot be named without making it a reflection, a phenomenon.

What the Others tell us about ourselves pertains only to our objectiveness: all that the Other can see is the Self. Therefore, when established in emancipated Being, without a Self, we are not susceptible to the Other's whims and biases. We are free to determine who we want to be. Furthermore, truly seeing each other we can transcend the Look towards essential Being—recognizing the Being behind the body, feelings, perception, ideas—and relate to each other in a more profound and realistic way.

When the body is clearly seen as not self, then it becomes poignantly clear that the importance we place on the color of the skin, the height, weight, and facial features are artificial and relative values, and we are less inclined to judge others and ourselves by them. Then we can avoid projecting ideas, feelings, and perceptions onto others. In this manner, we are mindful of the kamma that blinds us and become more perceptive of how our intentions affect and victimize others. Not that the ideal society should consist of individuals with communal clothing and stereotypical habits, but that personal differences should be regarded as superficial—with the fun and the lightness of a costume party.

When not identified with the Self, the Self we use to relate to each other is bound to be wholesome. The enlightened Being is necessarily good, for any action or intention which would be an affliction to others would in turn become an attachment to a Self and, therefore, a cause of suffering and not enlightenment. The natural state of Being is necessarily peaceful, happy, and benevolent.

# Conclusion

Gautama left the riches and comfort of his father's household and lived as a mendicant in quest of a method to end human suffering and to find a meaning for his own existence. After years of heroic meditation efforts, severe renunciation, and self-mortification, he finally became a perfectly enlightened being, a Buddha. He had reached his goal: The Unconditioned, the Unborn, true happiness and fulfilment, Nibbana. Now unbound from all aspects of Self, resting in plenitude, unmoved as a mountain, he needed nothing. So, what moved him to spend the following 45 years travelling as a mendicant teacher? It is said that he was moved by compassion for the suffering of others (MN 26). But what is compassion for a group of "aggregates", for a non-being? Isn't compassion already evidence of a transcendence of the physical? Of the apprehension of a real suffering person? The comprehension of another Being, there?

# Why Existential Buddhism

M any practitioners of Buddhism, both in the east and the west, believe that it is very difficult to become enlightened; that it is only possible for monks, or those who have exceptional time and talent. Many spend long hours in concentration meditation striving for a transcendental experience or a profound personal transformation. Those who do report having a transformative experience frequently relate that it is not lasting, and that they later continue to suffer from attachments and frustrations. The reason for these misperceptions and failures is due to a misunderstanding of the goal of the Not-self doctrine.

Existentialism is generally relegated to the history of philosophy. Finding nothing but absurdity in the Nothingness, philosophers returned to the comfort of reflection and logic. Sartre himself did not express much hope in finding an authentic resolution to the problem of Bad Faith; insisting that one must create one's essence, invent one's values. Although Heidegger revealed human essence as Dasein (the German term meaning for being-there), as the human experience of Being, the transcendent revelations of his work have not been generally appreciated.

Despite seeming different, Existentialism and Buddhism complement each other. Buddhism has been from its inception a pragmatic discipline for the liberation of the mind from suffering. While it has proven efficacious as a psychology, it relies on ancient metaphysical beliefs which no longer resonate with the modern mentality or lead to absurd or nihilistic interpretations, hence limiting its general appeal and acceptance. Existentialism, despite its concern with the problem of existence, lacks clear practical applications of its insights. Buddhism and Existentialism coincide in a foundation of Being. Like two sides of the same coin, it is from this axis that both disciplines complete each other.

The project of the Not-self doctrine is to identify everything which can be experienced, everything which can be thought of or observed, as other than oneself. This makes everything, all possible perception, an object of awareness. What is left of oneself in the fruition this insight is the pure awareness of existing, of Being. Existentialism elucidates how this Being is simultaneously not anything, as a Nothingness, and the source of everything.

Being is not anything; it is the negation of everything which can be perceived; it is, from the point of view or reason, a Nothingness. Human self-consciousness, as Being, has no substance: its essence is existence. In this sense, it is an emptiness, and since everything that can be experienced is a conscious experience (the phenomenon), then everything (all that exists) is empty as well. What is beyond conscious perception is also an emptiness because it is not subject to conceptualization, as any idea of what would be beyond is already an object of consciousness.

Being is the wellspring of our humanness. The visual, musical, and literary arts emerge from our ability to make sense of the world, from our existential apprehension, and our intrinsic inspiration. Our empathy, sense of justice, and deference for the truth stem from the freedom and meaningfulness of Being. We are more human the less we are the world: the more we are centered in Being.

To think, to read, to remember, to observe, to move the body, all require attention and mental effort, but to be conscious is spontaneous, requires no effort on our part. When the body and mind are exhausted from intense activity, your awareness does not decrease—you are not less conscious—you are just aware of being spent. To exist, to Be, is effortless.

With concentration meditation you can experience Being directly. When the mind is able to focus on the breathing unswervingly, then all thoughts and bodily perceptions give way to just an awareness of being aware. Although this experience is temporary, it becomes sufficient to identify the awareness as the Being, and the World as other. With practice and time, this discernment of existing as Being becomes established in and out of meditation. This is a home; this is a refuge; it is the path to liberation.

Because the nature of consciousness is a Nothingness, we can understand how Karma works. Because it has no essence, unenlightened mind becomes all the thoughts and emotions that it projects onto others. In other words, we are affected at once by the way we treat others. So, we become the anger we direct at others, and the kindness we treat others with. This is the true workings of Kamma (Karma), rather than the belief in some obscure cosmic force that parcels out retributions.

With the insights gained from Existentialism, we can better comprehend what occurs with Enlightenment and Unbinding (or Nibbana).

The enlightenment of Enlightenment has more to do with mentality than with anything else. If you have developed a habit of thinking too much, of worrying, of holding on to your World to feel secure, then when you finally let go of it, it will feel as if you were born again. If you have been chronically depressed, or angry, or overly sentimental, then you live with strong emotional attachments, and releasing your grip on these will make you feel like you have come close to heaven, light and peaceful. If you are generally easygoing and relaxed, where nothing really rocks your boat, then releasing the World will feel more natural, as a profound peacefulness, but without bells and whistles.

Enlightenment is not the conclusion of the effort to liberate the mind, it is not the final frontier. Understanding this is critical because many practitioners experience profound mental clarity and peacefulness after releasing the World and believe that this enlightenment is Liberation (or Nirvana); then become frustrated, depressed, and disenchanted, when the problems and stresses of the world, like dark clouds, come creeping back into the mind.

Enlightenment can be best understood as the realization of not being the World: the sudden realization of a point of view outside of the World. It is the awareness of the expulsion (nihilation) of the World from consciousness. Suddenly I apprehend that everything I see, everything I know, is not what I am, but are all objects of my awareness, and I am the emptiness of everything. We call Enlightenment the realization of this profound, all at once insight into the nature of human existence. We can call it Original Mind because it is the fundamental state of unencumbered consciousness; it is what awareness is before it becomes entangled with the World.

But even though I am the negation of the World as Not-self, as a Nothingness, I am not non-existence, for it is I, the individual being, who does the negating, the nihilation, through my existing in the world (as a first Ekstasis). This emptiness of the World which I am, I am as Being. This Being is the indubitable certitude of my existence, all at once unfathomably profound and terribly mundane. What makes Buddhism impenetrable for many, and makes many interpretations incomplete and unnecessarily esoteric, is the misunderstanding of the Not-self as a No-self doctrine, or as the consummation of the path; what becomes, rather, an attachment to negation. The Not-self doctrine opens the way to the realization of the awareness of the *absolute subjectivity* of human consciousness, which the Buddha left unnamed to maintain the exposition of this reality unambiguous: what I point to with Being. Without this apprehension of the Not-self doctrine, the realization of Buddhism is reduced to a contradiction: a non-existent point of view, a Nihilism.

In one famous sutta, the Buddha points directly to the Nothingness of human consciousness, as that which is beyond the World of conditioned things:

*There is, monks, an unborn — unbecome — unmade — unfabricated. If there were not that unborn — unbecome — unmade — unfabricated, there would not be the case that emancipation from the born — become — made — fabricated would be discerned. But precisely because there is an unborn — unbecome — unmade — unfabricated, that emancipation from the born — become — made — fabricated is discerned. (Ud 8.3) (Nibbana 2013)*

Which means that human consciousness must originate outside the world of conditioned things, must be unconditioned, for it to have awareness of conditioned things, and to be capable of procuring emancipation. This is consistent with Sartre's assessment of self-consciousness as being a nihilation of the world, of being as if at a distance from it.

Once Enlightened, then we can proceed to methodically cleanse the mind of all the bad habits and attachments we have accumulated in our life as Self. Any entity, which arises in the field of consciousness is something which we have created out of our contact with the world, is an impermanent condition, and is not Being. Ideas, beliefs, emotions, perceptions, and all I have created in my interaction with the world, all I can appreciate to come and go without my grasping them. As I do this more and more, I become increasingly centered in Being, in my awareness of existing.

Enlightenment is the beginning of our journey towards our emancipation in Being, towards Unbinding. Once we have that fundamental insight into the nature of our consciousness as not anything of the World, we can nurture it with ongoing mindfulness of everything we do in our daily routines. As the World becomes more Not-self, as we become further accustomed to not grasping the World, our Being becomes more discernible and unaffected.

What the Buddha called the Unbinding (Nibbana, in the Pali language, or Nirvana in Sanskrit), is that consciousness which has accomplished a complete emancipation from the World as Self: it is totally at peace and unmoved from its center in Being; here, there is a complete liberation from identification with a Self; here, there is total Freedom of mind and Authentic Happiness.

Human self-consciousness is always a nihilation of the World, which means that it is in essence Not-self—what some Buddhist schools refer to as the Original Mind. It is with this understanding that the Mahayana Buddhist insist that everyone is already a Buddha. Indeed, we come to self-consciousness in our early childhood through a nihilation of the world, and then we develop an attachment to the World as Self. It is this nihilation which allows us to apprehend the existence of the world, and it is the world that allows us to discern our own existence. Without the world, as Sartre says, we exist all at once: like a floodlight aimed into pure darkness—the light is undetected even though it does not cease to exist. We become individuals through our being in time and existing as a Self; albeit in this process we become entangled with the World. This is what we learn from Existentialism.

We suffer because we are not of the world, because as a nihilation of the world, we are left alien to it. We suffer because the Self that we embrace is a false Self—one we hold in Bad Faith. Our Nothingness constantly haunts our existence in the world, as no-thing can ever full-fill that emptiness. We are condemned to a life of lacking and exigencies, like Sisyphus absurdly rolling the rock up the hill, never finding rest. Yet, it is this Nothingness, this emptiness, which also motivates our search for true happiness, for autonomy, for true Freedom. When we learn to live undaunted by the World, then there is nothing to want, nothing to accomplish, nothing to become. We accept life as it comes. This is the end of suffering.

This Being has been called the Ordinary Mind, but there is nothing ordinary about it. Our consciousness of existence only appears unremarkable, ordinary, because it is the background to everything. But once we realize the true nature of the World as Not-self, then the extraordinary nature of our Being becomes gloriously evident. What I apprehend in my meditations, when all thoughts and all perceptions disappear, is that I am who gives everything in the world its existence, its sense of reality, its being there: Consciousness is not receptive of the World, but creative! A rose, for example, is exactly nothing in and of itself, it is I who makes its red petals, its green leaves, and its thorns real; it is I who makes it beautiful, poetic, and a symbol of love: it is I who calls it into being. It is in this sense that Being is what is most obvious, most abstruse, and most profound.

Existential Buddhism does not change the purpose and practice of traditional Buddhism. It rather substantiates and clarifies its principles to make the discipline and its realization more evident and accessible.

Existential Buddhism presents a wholistic and modern approach to the questions of existence. It provides for a congruent and effective method for achieving peace of mind, happiness, and authentic meaningfulness.

# Bibliography

Access to Insight. 2005. "Intentional action: *Kamma* (Skt: *karma*)."edited by Access to Insight. Access to Insight (Legacy Edition). November 5, 2013. Accessed August 3, 2016. http://www.accesstoinsight.org/ptf/dhamma/sacca/sacca4/samma-ditthi/kamma.html .

----2010."Anatta-lakkhana Sutta: The Discourse on the Not-self Characteristic" (SN 22.59), translated from the Pali by Ñanamoli Thera. *Access to Insight (BCBS Edition)*, 13 June 2010, http://www.accesstoinsight.org/tipitaka/sn/sn22/sn22.059.nymo.html .

----2013. "Jhana Sutta: Mental Absorption" (AN 9.36), translated from the Pali by Thanissaro Bhikkhu. *Access to Insight (BCBS Edition)*, 30 November 2013, http://www.accesstoinsight.org/tipitaka/an/an09/an09.036.than.html .

Ainsworth, M. D. S., Bell, S. M., and Stayton, D. J. 1971. *The Origins of Human Social Relations*. New York: Academic Press.


Bhikkhu, Thanissaro. 1996. "No-self or Not-self?" Access to Insight (Legacy Edition), November 24, 2010. Accessed September 10, 2015. http://www.accesstoinsight.org/lib/au-thors/thanissaro/notself2.html.

----.2011."MN 63." In "Selves and Not-self: The Bud-dhist Teaching on Anatta." Access to Insight (Legacy Edition) November 30, 2013. Accessed August 2, 2016. http://www.accesstoin-sight.org/lib/authors/thanissaro/selvesnot-self.html.

----.1997."Jhana Sutta: Mental Absorption" (AN 9.36). Translated from the Pali by Thanissaro Bhikkhu. Access to Insight (Legacy Edition), No-vember 30, 2013. Accessed August 3, 2016. http://www.accesstoinsight.org/tipi-taka/an/an09/an09.036.than.html.

----.1998. "Maha-salayatanika Sutta: The Great Six Sense-media Discourse" (MN 149). Translated from the Pali by Thanissaro Bhikkhu. Access to Insight (Legacy Edition) November 30, 2013. Ac-cessed August 8, 2016. http://www.accesstoin-sight.org/tipitaka/mm/mn.149.than.html .

----.1999. "Mind Like Fire Unbound: Introduction (Fourth Edition)." Thanissaro Bhikkhu (Geoffrey

DeGraff). Access to Insight (Legacy Edition) April 23, 2012. Accessed August 14, 2016. http://www.accesstoinsight.org/lib/authors/thanissaro/likefire/2-0.html.

----.2005. "A Verb for Nirvana." Thanissaro Bhikkhu. Access to Insight (Legacy Edition). June 5, 2010. Accessed August 14, 2016. http://www.accesstoinsight.org/lib/authors/thanissaro/nirvanaverb.html .

Blofeld, John. 1958. *The Zen Teachings of Huang Po: On the Transmission of Mind*. New York: Grove Press.

Bodhi, Bhikkhu. 2005. *In the Buddha's Words.* Boston: Wisdom Publication.

Buddharakkhita, Acharya. 1995. "Karaniya Metta Sutta: The Hymn of the Universal Love" (Sn 1.8). Translated from Pali by Acharya Buddharakkhita. Access to Insight (Legacy Edition). August 29, 2012. Accessed September 21, 2016. http://www.accesstoinsight.org/tipitaka/kn/snp.1.08.budd.html .

Buddhanet. 1996-2016. "The Heart Sutra: Prajna Paramita Hrydaya Sutra." http://www.buddhanet.net/e-learning/heartstr.html .

Chah, Ajahn. 2002. *Food for the Heart.* Massachu-
setts: Wisdom Publications.

Gerassi, John. 2009. *Talking with Sartre: Conversa-
tions and Debates.* Connecticut: Yale University.

Gunaratna, V.F. 1982. "Buddhist Reflections on
Death." Access to Insight (Legacy Edition). June
6, 2010. Accessed August 26, 2016. http://ac-
cesstoinsight.org/lib/au-
thors/gunaratna/wheel102.html .

Heidegger, Martin. 1962. *Being and Time.* Translated
by John Macquarrie and Edward Robinson. New
York: Harper and Row.

Jung, Carl. 1960. *On the Nature of the Psyche.* Translated by R. F. Hull. New Jersey: Princeton University Press.

Kornfield, Jack. 200. *After the Ecstasy, the Laundry.*
New York: Bantam Books.

Khema, Sister. 1984. "Meditating on No-Self: A Dhamma Talk (Edited for Bodhi Leaves)." Access toInsight (Legacy Edition), November 2, 2013. Accessed August 1, 2015. http://www.accesstoinsight.org/lib/authors/Khema/b1095.html .

Lockwood, Lewis. 2003. *Beethoven: the music and the life.* New York: W. W. Norton and company

Mendis, N.K.G. 1979. "On the No-self Characteristic: The Anatta-lakkhana Sutta"(SN 22.59). Translated by N.K.G. Mendis. Access to Insight (Legacy Edition), November 24, 2013. Accessed August 7,2016. http://www.accesstoinsight.org/lib/authors/mendis/wheel268.html .

Nhat Hanh, Thich. 2006. *Understanding Our Mind.* California: Parallax Press.

Mahathera, Nyanatiloka. 1984. "The Three Basic Facts of Existence: III. Egolessness (Anatta)." With a preface by Nanamoli Thera. Access to Insight (Legacy Edition), November 30, 2013. Accessed July 30, 2016. http://www.accesstoinsight.org/lib/authors/various/wheel202.html .

Sartre, Jean-Paul. 1984. *Being and Nothingness*. Translated by Hazel E. Barnes. New York: Washington Press.

----.2007. *Existentialism Is a Humanism*. Translated by Carol Macomber. New Haven: Yale University

Siegel, Daniel. 1999. *The Developing Mind: How Relationships and the Brain Interact to Shape Who We Are*. New York: The Gilford Press.

Solomon, Maynard. 1998. Beethoven. 2$^{nd}$ Rev. ed. New York: Schirmer Trade Books.

Sumedho, Ajahn. 1989. *The Way It Is.* Accessed August 6, 2016. http://www.amaravati.org/dhamma-books/the-way-it-is/ .

Tolle, Eckhart. 1999. *The Power of Now: A Guide to Spiritual Enlightenment.* California: New World Library.

Whitman, Walt. 1973. *The Portable Walt Whitman.* Edited by Mark Van Doren. New York: Penguin Books.

Wikipedia. 2004. "Das Lied von der Erde." Last modified September 1, 2016. Accessed September 21, 2016.                    https://en.wikipedia.org/wiki/Das_Lied_von_der_Erde

Wikipedia. 2005. "Immortal Beloved." Last modified
July 22, 2016. Accessed September 21, 2016.
https://en.wikipedia.org/wiki/Immortal_Beloved

# Appendix

# Anatta-lakkhana Sutta: The Discourse on the Not-self Characteristic

### translated from the Pali by Ñanamoli Thera

Thus I heard. On one occasion the Blessed One was living at Benares, in the Deer Park at Isipatana (the Resort of Seers). There he addressed the bhikkhus of the group of five: "Bhikkhus." — "Venerable sir," they replied. The Blessed One said this.

"Bhikkhus, form is not-self. Were form self, then this form would not lead to affliction, and one could have it of form: 'Let my form be thus, let my form be not thus.' And since form is not-self, so it leads to affliction, and none can have it of form: 'Let my form be thus, let my form be not thus.'

"Bhikkhus, feeling is not-self...

"Bhikkhus, perception is not-self...

"Bhikkhus, determinations are not-self...

"Bhikkhus, consciousness is not self. Were consciousness self, then this consciousness would not lead to affliction, and one could have it of consciousness: 'Let my consciousness be thus, let my consciousness be not thus.' And since consciousness is not-self, so it leads to affliction, and none can have it of consciousness: 'Let my consciousness be thus, let my consciousness be not thus.'

"Bhikkhus, how do you conceive it: is form permanent or impermanent?" — "Impermanent, venerable Sir." — "Now is what is impermanent painful or pleasant?" — "Painful, venerable Sir." — "Now is what is impermanent, what is painful since subject to change, fit to be regarded thus: 'This is mine, this is I, this is my self'"? — "No, venerable sir."

"Is feeling permanent or impermanent?...

"Is perception permanent or impermanent?...

"Are determinations permanent or impermanent?...

"Is consciousness permanent or impermanent?"
— "Impermanent, venerable sir." — "Now is what
is impermanent pleasant or painful?" — "Painful,
venerable sir." — "Now is what is impermanent,
what is painful since subject to change, fit to be
regarded thus: 'This is mine, this is I, this is my
self'"? — "No, venerable sir."

"So, bhikkhus any kind of form whatever, whether
past, future or presently arisen, whether gross or
subtle, whether in oneself or external, whether inferior or superior, whether far or near, must with
right understanding how it is, be regarded thus:
'This is not mine, this is not I, this is not myself.'

"Any kind of feeling whatever...

"Any kind of perception whatever...

"Any kind of determination whatever...

"Any kind of consciousness whatever, whether
past, future or presently arisen, whether gross or

subtle, whether in oneself or external, whether inferior or superior, whether far or near must, with right understanding how it is, be regarded thus: 'This is not mine, this is not I, this is not my self.'

"Bhikkhus, when a noble follower who has heard (the truth) sees thus, he finds estrangement in form, he finds estrangement in feeling, he finds estrangement in perception, he finds estrangement in determinations, he finds estrangement in consciousness.

"When he finds estrangement, passion fades out. With the fading of passion, he is liberated. When liberated, there is knowledge that he is liberated. He understands: 'Birth is exhausted, the holy life has been lived out, what can be done is done, of this there is no more beyond.'"

That is what the Blessed One said. The bhikkhus were glad, and they approved his words.

Now during this utterance, the hearts of the bhikkhus of the group of five were liberated from taints through clinging no more. (*Access to Insight 2010*)

Made in the USA
Monee, IL
25 September 2021

78752656R00069